**'Welkam Ruhl Haus'**

Cover Design: Donna M. Kshir and Lee Roberts

Senior Editor: John Ruhl

Publisher: Welkam Ruhl Haus

Contact: authormaureenruhl@gmail.com

# SMOKE AND MIRRORS


MAUREEN A. RUHL

# Introduction:

I was approached by concerned citizens who heard rumors that a natural gas to electric power plant was coming to town. There were rumors throughout the community but only certain factions were available to the complete information and details of the project. The people who were in the know, were the project investors. They also put in place people who would see the project through to completion. But they did not anticipate a small group of town residents who actually would research the power plant and uncover small town corruption, at many levels.

This group of four visited three surrounding power plant towns in Shamokin Dam, Montgomery and Jessup, Pennsylvania. It became clear that the power plant would not bring the town prosperity but only financially benefit  the 49 investors. The fear of the investors manifested at an informational rally, organized by the concerned citizens. The rally was attended by the investors, politicians,  media and union organizers. They created chaos, talked over the qualified speakers, hijacked Facebook and social media and the newspaper printed an inflammatory and biased piece.

Most people may have retreated but not the members of this group! They found renewed strength and grew in numbers! They were emboldened by the tactics used by the pro power plant followers. The situation reeked of desperation and greed, a last chance effort on their part to recoup lost revenue. The land the power plant was to be built upon, was filled with toxic waste, which was not identified in the soil testing phase. If this plant were to be built on this land, every homeowner would have a power plant within a football field of their home. Many homes that are well over a hundred years old and built upon the town's fractured infrastructure, with several buildings already leveled and many more in distress.

The power plant promises were distortions of truth and created to mislead. Their written promises were nothing more than the federal minimum requirements.

*Maureen*

# Smoke and Mirrors:

Renovo is more of a hamlet than a town, with around 1,200 residents. It was formed by the now defunct Pennsylvania Railroad. It was the midpoint between New York City , N. Y. and Erie, Pennsylvania.

The town grew out of the mountains as naturally as the streams, rivers seemed to fill in the creases and valleys. Teeming with wildlife and the abundance of natural falls, the town of Renovo grew to encapsulate a growing tanning industry, brick making forges and of course lumber! The lumber once harvested was sent down the mountains through the streams and eventually the West Branch of the Susquehanna river. The lumber reached its final destinations down river to Lock Haven and Williamsport! Yes, Renovo thrived by repairing and building railroad cars and spirited rides of transportation throughout the growing United States. Railroads connected the majority of towns and cities of commerce and trade. The town grew as the jobs became bountiful and the pay was good enough to leave other countries behind in the exodus! Italy, Ireland, Europe all pioneers looking for a new start and opportunities in burgeoning new industries! The great railroad was the place to work for it invited all forms of talent from upholstery, welding, metal forming and servicing the tracks, to greet customers and baggage carriers! Some workers traveled the country while others still grew their families up and down the streets. As the town expanded it stretched into the nooks and crannies of the mountains and started villages in East Renovo, South Renovo, Westport, Kettle Creek, North Bend and Farwell, to mention a few! The railroads were the lifeline of a growing nation and to fuel this endeavor they needed to be supported by Pennsylvania's large coal deposits and ample water supply. This was a time well before the environmentalists, when the forests could be made barren and streams could be polluted, mines were carved by any enterprising individuals without regard to stripping the earth of its black gold, without any care or consequence. The town was filled with the smells of delicious cuisines, from the busy kitchens of Italian grandmas, Welch, Irish and European immigrants all adding their flavors! Thickened stews, tomato sauces, baked breads and distinct spices, wafted through open screen doors and snaked their way through the hamlets! The sound of children laughing and playing in the alleys and backyards, as children were kept busy with balls, sticks and fishing poles! This of course after they completed their chores! Families were large and the work was made easier with many hands sharing the duties!

There were clothes to wash, meals to prepare, beds to make and siblings to keep a watchful eye on! Hard work at the mines, tanneries, railroad shops and lumber companies indeed created an appetite for great food and great fun! These hard working, new arrivals to America wanted to provide their families with joys and freedoms that they never experienced. The freedom to choose prosperity over poverty, the freedom to worship in the faith of their choice and the pride which they wore as they embraced the individualism of being an American!

This America created prosperity for those who worked hard and were disciplined! Pride was earned and respected by the stripes of sweat across the brow and honor was displayed in being truthful and honorable in their daily transactions with one another. There were the occasional entanglements of the flesh, when one drank too much at a bar and clobbered his best friend but afterward, they shook hands and all was forgotten. Debts made were repaid and folks saved for things like their first house and their children's education. Nothing was spontaneous, not even gratification. All was earned, day by day, week by week. The government did not meddle in the lives of people or intrusively overstep their authority. The playing field was even for everyone to participate and thrive, if they have the determination and gumption to succeed. Because of the plentiful jobs, individuals could easily find work and without the distractions of televisions and computers, many chose to marry and create families of their own! It was the logical step to grow the family as they prospered and they cherished family above all else, except God. Faith, fellowship and human kindness was thriving because if a family needed help, it was the family responsibility to ensure safety. They were backed up by the church and charity was looked upon as something reverent, not expected.

The railroad expanded across the country and provided many exotic destinations! Cities like Chicago and Philadelphia were now accessible and the train made it practical for shopping trips and visiting far away relatives! There were even offers of work and attending universities that were never before even contemplated, much less, within one's reach! The railroad definitely created new dreams and adventures ,unsurpassed in America's history but the world would take a violent and unexpected turn towards world war and the romance of the railroad would suffer. The workhorse of war was the railroad, carrying dizzying amounts of coal, steel, components of every kind, shape, size and of course, people. Transportation was in its heyday and Renovo was thriving! The railroad was growing exponentially and the jobs were plentiful! The town grew and churches bulged with prayers and they supported efforts for the war. War is always a somber time and yet there is always faith to sustain us and hold us steady. Churches and synagogues are the strong oaks holding up society when the frailty of the human spirit is destroyed by greed and power.

As the world finished its savagery and worldwide destruction, the world was charting a new course, a road where the railroad could no longer compete. Because as the world had just been opened and occupied by these young men and women, they longed for new roads to travel and discover. No longer content with the roads traveled by rail but the new roads being constructed throughout America, leading to little towns, and unknown locations. Detroit was producing cars and trucks enthusiastically but the appetite for four wheeled freedom was ferocious! The railroad would still be an important component in transportation but it had lost its romance and financial footing. Renovo's biggest employer was slipping into oblivion and along with it, all its supporting industries. A dark storm had now fallen upon Renovo, its residents and there was no silver lining. Once a bustling railroad town, with shops, taverns, barber shops, bakeries and mom and pop stores were now shuttered. People who had spent their lives here raising their families, now had to look for employment elsewhere. Just as the lumber shops, tanning and brick forges fell into obscurity, so had Renovo. Attempts were made over the years to bring new life and breath to Renovo but those efforts dissolved as soon as a profit was made and the investors fled! It was easy to sell dreams to a town who once believed in them but to a new generation that only knew hard times, decaying properties and opportunities out of reach, this was clearly Renovo's new reality. It was bleak as a cancer diagnosis and just as harmful. Once a town loses its viability its people lose their vitality. For many years the railroad field stood empty and was at one point a keystone opportunity zone. But then at some point, the land came into private ownership.

There could not have been a more eclectic group of people who came together to protest the power plant. It consisted of a life long, sixty something resident and great grandma, a thirty something tattoo artist, who returned to town from life around the globe, a retired veteran and ecology activist, a retired English professor and a government watchdog, who really acted more like a bulldog! When she got her teeth around a good factoid, she held onto it for dear life! The community was being told the same, tired promises that every prospective energy company panders to the towns they begin to hover. They look for distressed towns who are in great need of a financial shot in the arm! They wine and dine the politicians, they flap their snake oiled tongues to the business owners and sprinkle their magic dust upon the unsuspecting, while transforming themselves into the epic answer to prosperity!

This routine, they have eloquently repeated time and time again! Their efficiency and execution are exact with precision! They promise large tax revenue, when in fact they resist to pay their fair share and school districts must sue to get what they are rightfully owed.The fire companies are promised new equipment and the municipality is promised investment in local infrastructure. The tongues continue to wag and the ears of willing listeners are hanging onto every word! Their audience is handpicked and selected members within the community who are most susceptible to swallowing their empty promises. They, unknowingly, will also be the ones who will force feed these promises to fellow citizens.They have no idea that their quest for economic prosperity will consume them with greed. The land owners do not have a successful track record of business superiority. In fact the land was used as a dump where other businesses discarded their waste, before environmental laws were enacted. The power plant has also promised to clean up the brownfield ,but will they clean up the toxicity 80 feet below? Trees and grass do not grow upon the soil, either! This is the location chosen by the power plant? The railroad land owners desperately need to sell this land. They have investors that lost money on their previous business ventures and they feel this is their last chance! Whether it is or not, should those people be able to alter an entire community, place a power plant upon toxic ground and within feet of residents homes? The investors are individuals who at the time they invested, they thought it was a great investment and for a while received dividends! But then the business closed and their dreams of profits died. Or did it? Perhaps, selling the land to the power plant was part two of their business plan, all along. Maybe it wasn't a stroke of luck or divine intervention that lured the power plant to Renovo. The idea of putting a power plant in Renovo was on the drawing board about the time the first business closed and negotiations have been going on for six years. A lot of activity that goes on at an LLC in Pennsylvania is confidential but there is always a paper trail. Several of us scoured through thousands of documents, land transfers, DEP, DCNR and EPA reports, borough minutes, grants and timelines that created a clearer picture of what was going on! Obviously, when a power plant comes to town it represents itself as a prophet, proclaiming good works. There is a feel good message when you are on the receiving end of increased personal wealth and promised contracts. And there is a lot of work to be done, when building a billion dollar power plant! The work contracts are completed by crews who specialize in particular aspects of the huge puzzle. There are water and sewer lines to be laid, buildings to erect, components to attach. Miles of electric wires to run, turbines, towers and computers to set up, offices, bathrooms, laboratories and clean rooms, to mention a few! The hopeful local contractors are anxious to pick up crumbs that fall from the negotiating table. They look for any opportunity, nuance or opening, so they can be a part of the project. However, the power plant prophets are highly aware of their desperation, that is why they were chosen to participate in the process. Besides the land owners and politicians, who hope to reap dividends and increased taxes, without much effort. The contractors stand to gain financial opportunities only if they fight for it. And fight they must!

The power plant negotiators are astute and have the instinct of a hunter. They clearly know their prey, smell their fear and set the trap. They owe their allegiance, not to the towns, or the levels of government agencies but to their stockholders!

Energy is a product, a commodity, not unlike widgets but energy is manufactured in locations carefully selected for their exploitation. It's a nasty game of want and take. They want easy access to natural resources, pick up the location for pennies on the dollar and transform the area into the domain of the power plant. This is not the kingdom of princes on white horses, no it becomes the castle of the bad king, complete with a surveillance drawbridge. The town is held captive to the energy management process where electricity reigns supreme. Pulsing through the remotely controlled, computer complex, is the electric grid. Each kilowatt has a price tag and the city who pays the most wins! It only takes seconds to redirect electricity from New York city to Chicago and those seconds calculate into astronomical financial rewards!

Why are power plants being built in Pennsylvania to serve other states? Well that's where the politicians make their contribution! You see, states like New York, want to sound progressive and tell their statesman that the electricity they are purchasing is "clean". That's code for hey, we don't pollute our state by making electricity! No, it is up to the governor and legislators of Pennsylvania to sell out our state forests, game lands and streams. And if you think that's crazy, well wait, because they "sell" carbon credits, as well! Carbon credits do not exist; they are a figment of governments imagination. They sell these credits to power plants who pollute more than the law allows but it's not perceived as an infraction of law. Oh my no! Power plants buy these credits from the state and the state can proclaim they care about the environment, while collecting carbon credit donations! If only the average businessman could sell you a head cold and then sell you the cure! The government has lost their direction, their compass is spinning frantically and they have lost their responsibility calibration. After Pennsylvania spent hundreds of millions of dollars to clean up the streams, replenish forests, restore ecological balance, they sold out to the power plant industry.

Our town was founded by the Pennsylvania Railroad, which I mentioned earlier. We have benefited greatly and suffered miserably by the rise and fall of the railroad. The power plant promises to bring prosperity, once again but I hesitate to believe their words. For one thing, they have promised to bring cutting edge technology but the plans they submitted for approval are not the newest generation. They have promised investment in our town but so far the town has gone into debt and obtained grants and loans for infrastructure improvements which will primarily benefit the power plant. We have been promised employment opportunities but most of the jobs have already been awarded. They have promised our homes will increase in value but who will want to buy a home feet away from an operating power plant? Most of our residents are retired senior citizens and just want to grow old here. Simple things like sitting on the porch, hanging wash on the line, leaving windows open to capture the pure mountain air, will not be possible once the plant is operating.

 The lights around the plant will illuminate our town 24/7. The constant hum of the turbines will affect our noise level. The vibrations will have a direct effect on humans as well as our wildlife. Every business considers its location above all other considerations. However, Renovo has a piece of property, smack dab in the center of town. It is home to the railroad tracks that sneak their way from points east to west.. The strip of land is narrow and long, with the railroad tracks to the south and the foot of the mountains to the north. The propaganda printed and distributed by the power plant shows the power plant as cute as a picture on a postcard! But they have enlarged the plant after the size was approved! We visited other power plants and they do not fit into the existing space. The stacks at our plant will rise 246 feet to be above the mountain top, whereas other plant stacks are 50 feet high. There is a public use road, in case of emergency or flooding, that will run right through the proposed footprint of the plant. How will they maintain security of the plant if the road is ever opened? Security will be paramount and understandably so because of the risks in our world today.

The thing I have heard over and over is how remarkable the town of Renovo Pennsylvania is to its people. So much so that many return here to retire and live out their final years surrounded by the forests, mountains and the West Branch of the Susquehanna river which fueled their younger days! They grew up in the forties, fifties and sixties, as close knit families, where Sunday mornings were spent at church, followed by big family dinners afterward. Some families had ten or twelve children but they never knew hunger or realized that hand me downs were out of fashion. The economy of Renovo was thriving, with shops, bakeries, several grocery stores and restaurants. Jobs were plentiful at the railroad or its supporting industries. There was a movie theater, bowling alley, swimming pool and even a country club! Gas was cheap so driving out of Renovo and venturing into the college town of Lock Haven, created even more opportunities. And education was the real equalizer. Jobs were available right out of high school but many also chose to pursue higher education or stints in the military, to quench their fever for adventure or even better job opportunities. While parents and many siblings stayed behind and made their lives within the boundaries of Renovo, even those who had left, knew they wanted to return, one day. Transportation was changing in the sixties and by the seventies, the railroads future was doomed. Tractor trailers could load up at ocean ports and with the evolution of the interstates, carry cargo to any street address. This was the flaw in rail service, where the cargo could get close to the final destination but not up to the loading dock. Passengers who once were treated as royalty on the passenger trains, were now opting to travel cross country instead in their own family car. Detroit was now specializing in making automobiles desired by everyone, no matter their taste! The world was focused on the 'space race' and cars were re-imagined with fins, chrome and gigantic horse power! A driver could now feel the pulse of the engine through the steering wheel and accelerate by tapping the floor pedal. Add to that the speed gear shift stick and everyone imagined themselves a pilot! No longer satisfied with rail luxury, they wanted to own their own four wheeled style of luxury!

The world was changing, traditional war was growing weary upon the people and energy was becoming the new commodity waging war. The seventies brought barrels of oil and refineries to near crisis levels. Barrel costs rose to never before seen prices and gas stations were forced to ration and the long lines were on the nightly news. The middle east countries, once seen only as backward deserts, were quickly becoming first world countries. And the wealth they flouted was embarrassing. The

United States of America was caught off guard and unprepared for the new oil barons, who banded together and created a forum to set prices, OPEC. The realization of the utter importance of our natural resources was finally revealed. Without constant and renewable energy resources at our disposal and under control of the US government, we would be helpless in this new world.

An inventory of sorts was taken and scientists recorded all resources, giving prominence to solar, nuclear and wind turbines above ground, as well as coal, gas and natural gas below the surface. Renovo was Blessed with natural gas reserves and now their importance would become imminent. Fracking, a new technology to probe and inject water and chemicals into natural gas pockets, looked promising! This technology could increase the speed and efficiency of extracting the gas and continue the exploitation of our land. In the haste to harvest this resource, the chemicals and water caused some unforeseen dangers. The profits for landowners who rented out their land for fracking, quickly realized that with quick rich schemes comes tragedy. Wells which provided drinking water for their family and animals were being poisoned. It was not deliberate but by intentionally using a new technology, without proper vetting, caused irreparable harm. And as quickly as the fracking companies came to town, they left. They left in haste, leaving unpaid debts, tainted wells and they left no recourse for the victims.

Energy companies fall under protections by the very government that is to serve its citizens. And these protections provided are paid for by the citizens. In some cases ,the citizens are victims of the energy companies and then have the indignity of paying taxes, which the government uses to pay off the energy companies. It is mind boggling and not a fair playing field. The government is trying to secure its energy independence but bypasses some of its own laws to do so. There are many environmental laws enforced by the Department of Environmental Protection, Environmental Protection Agency and state agencies such as the Department of Conservation and Natural Resources. Surely, these enforcement arms of the government can ensure the safety of its citizens? The answer comes down to revenue. If the state gains revenue by increased taxes, they will bend the environmental laws to ensure increased revenue. Government enjoys the appearance of protecting the planet but the reality is that environmental laws are not obeyed with regularity. These laws are stretched, manipulated, formed and re-designed at the whim of politicians. Look at ANY law that is written to protect the planet and you will find variations and objectives but not clarity. These indecisive and confusing laws are written only for appearance sake.

They are missing substance and thus have no teeth. For a government that is built on law and order, we have failed the planet. Environmental law is in its infancy and has generations to define its mission and make its laws serious, merited and instill discipline in its enforcement. Until those things happen, I do not trust that the spirit of the law will be enacted or enforced and that should give pause to everyone. We as a people perform best when we know the perimeters of our freedom and can count on consequences for those who do not respect that freedom. We have come to expect a bending of our laws by politicians but must we accept the blatant disregard of those laws? Each of us has a responsibility to bring no harm to everything and everyone we interact with. So why is it a stretch to expect the same from our government? I know we cannot avoid all harmful situations but we should expect our government to steer clear of the most obvious obstructions. And we should expect that there are consequences for those who actively pollute, poison or negatively transform our planet. I believe that most of us are focused on doing our part to recycle, stop littering, reduce trash and repurpose items before throwing them away. We consolidate, identify and sort items as to their worth, should we not do the same with attention to our worth?

The value of our children certainly requires us to provide them with a cleaner planet. One that has a smoke-free and chemical-free atmosphere. One that includes pesticide-free food and poison-free water. We know the dangers of not following these rules and yet governments continue to bend those rules for the sake of money.

Greed is what is currently driving the natural gas to electric power plants, not empathy, as some would like to claim! Are we more patriotic when we place a power plant on toxic land and generate electricity for far away cities? Is it gratuity that propels someone to sell their town for the prospect of increased revenue? Renovo has had its soul stolen and bartered away for a few silver coins. In fact, the story of this corruption started many years prior when two copies of three copies of a Department of Environmental Protection report went missing! The report clearly stated that the soil was contaminated in several communities but the report was ordered to be destroyed! One copy exists because of the rare and priceless gift of one woman's compassion for her fellow neighbors. She knew that destroying the report would be paramount to allowing the residents to be unprotected and vulnerable. She knew what vulnerability and victimization felt like because in her lifetime she had borne the brunt of it. Her life was not easy. She had been the victim of intimidation, sexual assault and the mother of disabled children. Just one of these travesties would have been sufficient to change her outlook on life but with several calamities combined, she was inundated with a lifetime of pain and hardship. And yet, her compassion remained and she held onto a report she was directed to destroy. Her life was hard and yet she made the proper decision. So many people today have hardships or struggles and they play the pity me card. They flash that card every time life gets difficult or they feel a twinge of pain. But this woman rose through all her challenges and put herself at risk, potential physical harm and risk of death, to sound the alarm for her neighbors! She realized that the contamination would impact her community in various and unholy ways. Illness, disease, birth defects and death. Why would anyone destroy a report that could sound a warning to these truths? How could a government report in which many people collaborated, just disappear? It seems almost impossible and yet this is the truth. I do not understand the level of malice that resides within an individual, capable of putting thousands of lives at risk, for the intended purpose to get rich. To them, life is a game and the one with the most money wins! But what do they gain if they jeopardize the lives of others in their obsession of securing wealth? I will never understand the need to harm others. Are they really any different than a murderer, who uses a gun or knife to slay their victims? Isn't the potential poisoning of several communities a crime? Isn't the result the same? Lives are taken over time, one by one, with various ailments set in motion by the arrogance and absolute callousness of a few highly respected individuals. Individuals who are looked upon with reverence in the community and respect. But these individuals thrive on their deception and are immune to public exposure. That is until their secrets are exposed and then they go running for cover. They seek absolution, convincing themselves they are not guilty of anything and go about counting their money. I seek restoration of the contaminated soil, as identified in the destroyed DEP report. For our waters to be restored to priestliness! None of us can survive without water, it is the lifeline within each of us. Even the wealthiest man or woman among us must have clean water to exist. Our planet demands little from us as trustees and yet we can't even muster the courage to treat it well. Preserve its natural habitat, encourage wildlife, protect streams, honor trees and serve it by doing no harm. But we have brought harm and indignation upon the very planet we were entrusted. The investors of the old railroad land are also negotiating the sale of toxic land to the Energy plant. Some investors also serve on local boards and on county commissions involved in bringing the power plant to Renovo. I would think that if a project brings you personal financial rewards, then you are not working for the benefit of the town citizens but for yourself. It should probably be against the law to serve on these committees when preparing your own personal financial gains. I was always told you can't serve two masters. A way around this obstacle is to "sell" the benefits to an unsuspecting audience and manipulate the political environment. This is a finely tuned tool, in the box of tricks, of the energy plant! They start by simply listening to the community leaders and with the full knowledge of the desperation they are sharing. The power plant deliberately selects communities because of their need for help. They select communities drowning in debt, decay and decades of neglect.

It is difficult to save a community with virtually no new tax dollars and few new ideas. Although the cement in between the bricks of the buildings is crumbling and the wooden supports bow, a town is so much more than its buildings. Structural and architectural features are but a small fraction of the total sum of a community. But their distress adequately displays its age. Homes in need of a fresh coat of paint, rusting spouting and weakening porches, bring another level of need to the equation. Once tidy, freshly painted and cared for homes are now screaming out for their saving grace and restoration.

But when a city suffers the atrocities of neglect and the perpetual can is kicked down the road, the residents become despondent. It is up to the community leaders to assist its residents but this can only become attained when the work is done in conjunction with its people, not in opposition to it. And so it was that the people who were voted to serve its residents, ended up in opposition to them. It was a subtle, silent change, driven by good intentions and promises of prosperity. Well, that is really up for each to determine on their own because the contempt that oozes from this no win situation, wreaks havoc on everyone. There is a huge emotional toll that is taken upon its residents. And instead of offering relief or offers of help, the people are blamed for their inequities. Their subsistence acknowledged and need for compassion is circumvented by nothing less than selfishness.

The two words that excite politicians like none other are jobs and increased taxes! The energy company charlatan brings these two ideas on a silver platter and serves them up to a starved audience. The promises are laden with delicacies and are eagerly eaten up with vigorous appetite! And the promise of jobs, even though unrealistic and are gobbled up like Thanksgiving Day turkey! The charlatan is very engaging, entertaining and enlightens everyone over to his way of thinking. He is after all, selling the promises of gluttony and greed. And as the people gorge on the feast of promises they are swiftly swallowing the hope of prosperity. It goes down easy, as a fine wine, served chilled, over ice. Human instinct is to follow the path of least resistance. As played in a child's game, it requires no effort to simply follow the leader. The leader is the one who has eloquently laid the groundwork and unleashed a half educated but full bellied crowd loose to continue to sell the message to the masses. Who can deny the lure and romanticism of a well paid job and the prospect of new tax dollars? Surely not politicians or their servants because with the hope of money in their pockets, they begin to sell the promises of the power plants to their constituents. But what they have failed to realize is that they should have reviewed the facts for themselves instead of blindly following the leader.

Now, not only have they fallen short of their obligations to voters but they also appear foolish. It is not easy to realize that you have been gullible and complacent in your duties of office. Politicians who cannot apologize and set the record straight are doomed to languish in ineptitude for eternity. All of us make mistakes and get lazy from time to time but we do expect our leaders to be perfect. They are not. They can come back from mistakes and be remade but to sign on to an idea that is not proved or investigated is a bit shameful. There is a whole world of experts on any topic, at the tip of our fingers. A few clicks of a keyboard can put the experts literally in our hands! That is why it is quite disturbing to find out this step of verification was ignored. I don't understand how someone can sell an idea that is not verified but only because it sounds good. I therefore cannot comprehend how people are driven to believe in the unbelievable. They continue to believe in the fantastical and with unbridled passion! Everyone seemingly wants to earn more money, get a better job or have an envious life. However, at what cost? Is it okay to sell out your friends and neighbors in pursuit of your own financial gains? Are you considered a savvy entrepreneur or just plain old greedy? These questions are relevant in today's world because we are supposed to be at the height of our intelligence beyond all previous generations. Sadly, it seems when it comes to greed, it rears its ugly head in every civilization. When it comes to money, we never have enough and always want more. The voters were denied a chance to register their opinion. When a power plant comes to town, the residents of that community should be offered a chance to vote. It is coming into their town and will directly affect their homes, lives and families. No outside pressure should be exerted or intimidation exercised upon them. Full disclosure by each opposing side should be provided to be evaluated. This includes politicians who are selling the benefits of the power plant, especially when they are not residents of that community! Recently a state representative said,"good things are coming to Renovo!" But I noticed she did not elaborate or identify what these good things will be. The local governing body should be impacted by facts and reality, not hopes and dreams. In our case they neglected their duties to do the research and simply rubber stamped what they were advised by the "experts". Our state governmental departments like the Department of Environmental Resources, DEP, are considered experts. The same department that let a report go "missing". The same ones ensure our safety and environmental health. They need to do their jobs thoroughly. There was one public meeting held but the meeting was packed with investors. Anyone with a personal financial stake in the project should have been identified. In that way, true concerned citizens, there for information gathering, could have been fairly counted. The general feeling of the DEP, at that meeting, was that the public was in favor of the power plant project, because they go on feelings rather than actual data. Investors should somehow be mathematically categorized so that data could be assessed and evaluated without prejudice. The meeting was held toward the beginning of the regulation process and that seems correct but there should have been at least one more public meeting toward the end of the regulation process because the process takes several years. In Renovo's case, many investors have passed, others have realized that some of the power plant promises are not true and they now decided that they do not want a power plant so close to their homes. Investors who do not live in Renovo have inflicted their heavy handed influence by providing funding and grants, making improvements which directly benefit Bechtel Energy. Why is it a community's financial responsibility to lay the groundwork for a company? Renovo needs police protection (we only have 30 hours a month at this time), infrastructure, entry level jobs, help with our drug problem and job training programs. Bechtel Energy knows how disenfranchised Renovo's economy is, it is one of the reasons they chose Renovo! So how can they in good conscience expect Renovo to pay for their entrance to Renovo? We need a federal investigation into the acts and actions of our local, county and state officials. Conflict of interest is only the beginning of the irregularities that are currently taking place. Please help!

The investors are a group of local businessmen and women, teachers, locals who were flush with retirement cash or family money, who thought they would back an idea to refurbish rail-cars. It sounded like a feasible plan and with a minimum investment of $10,000.00, it was relatively easy to find willing partners. The business plan must have sounded good but apparently poorly executed. After being in business for only a few years, the contracts stopped and investment dollars were lost. Most investors would have accepted their loss, licked their wounds and moved on. But the owners of the railroad business continued to entice prospective buyers of the industrial land and looked high and low for a business with deep pockets. And to further invite prospective buyers, the now closed railroad business, continued to advertise on Dun and Bradstreet as a business with sales of 1.6 million dollars and 24 employees. In fact six years after its bankruptcy, the truth was actively being misconstrued. Why would a bankrupt and closed business falsely advertise itself? You see, the old railroad property was not just contaminated with oil, diesel, grease, paint thinners and other industrial products. There was another secret they were hiding, 55 gallon barrels of toxic chemicals and buried waste. There was a chemical company operating on this property for a few years, another get rich quick scheme that was to bring jobs and prosperity to Renovo. But after a couple years of operation, they closed up and left. But not before they buried more secrets below the ground. The Pennsylvania Department of Environmental Protection (DEP) is supposed to clean up these sites and restore the environment. They are to follow the state's own environmental laws and enforce them properly. However, the dispensing of these regulations, has a bit to be desired. In fact, there are many instances, validated by emails and other correspondence, where DEP and government officials have directly issued permits in direct violation with DEP laws. They issued permits before verifying that all required regulations were met! Remember the "missing" DEP report, it detailed the high levels of contamination to the water and soil. The contamination was caused by years of inadequate sewer disposal and the soil was not able to be cleaned up without addressing the sewer problem. E-coli, fecal matter and a number of bacteria made the water and soil a health concern. However, by making the report disappear, the sewerage issues continued to be unresolved and another secret was buried. Renovo has been the continuous victim of cut and run, get rich quick schemes. The very railroad which built the town, also caused the town to be on life support, once it closed. And a few gallant attempts were made to bring jobs here but they were not well researched or executed, which all lead to failure. The local county and state government stepped in and brought tax incentives, free interest loans and other resources to bear, to locate and build businesses in Renovo.

But after these businesses close their doors, all the help they accepted, is never mentioned again, nor repaid. Sadly, this circle of building hope and bringing promises is followed by deceit, secrecy, and in the end, bankruptcy.

Renovo's buildings and roads are decaying slowly. Its people are struggling to keep their heads above the tides of old age and the young deal with deadly addictions. The Salvation Army and others provide food boxes, which are distributed weekly and monthly. The number of families in need continues to grow and multiply. The Covid-19 epidemic has brought unnecessary burdens of its own. Many of our citizens are longing for job opportunities and a ray of sunshine to light their path. Panderers are eager to supply false hope and empty promises. They have done so many times before. The United States of America has the promise of freedom of speech, free and fair elections! But when there is an unfinished job to be done, as in the case of selling private property to the energy company, the change of politicians at this time could be disastrous! And that was exactly the case on one particular election day! The stage was set for one lone candidate who was against the sale of the toxic land to the power company, to face off against the current council members who wanted the power plant. The reason against the power plant was simply, location. The land was set in the middle of town and would put a power plant within a football field of every residents' homes. The only reason this land was chosen to be sold was because of the greed of the investors! Over and over again they are heard to say, "this is our last chance to get some of our money back!" They also try the tactic of telling the residents it will be good for them! Ha! The residents know that a power plant, yards away from their homes, is not a good idea. Besides, Renovo is surrounded by thousands of acres of land up for sale, some even closer to the natural gas and river resources. And it would allow the power plant an extra margin of safety, built miles away, secluded and secure. On this election day, the air was crisp and tension lukewarm. The candidates up for reelection stood together, even with the gentleman who was running against the current mayor! It should be noted that the mayor gave a consolation speech at September's council meeting. So, was the placing of a new mayor, who also was an investor, part of the plan to close the deal? It makes sense because throughout this whole journey of researching the major players in this game, some names and their far reaching power extends to decimate the average citizen. The power plant will bring hundreds of union jobs to the area but not hire locals. And while the price of basic needs increases out of reach of the average person's stagnant wages or fixed income, all will be in direct competition for housing and food. This is over the short term of two to three years. After the workers leave ,the power plant will be in charge of purchasing water and natural gas and in huge volumes!

Who do you think will be able to easily pay skyrocketing costs? The average family? But beyond that, the town will return to its original state of decay. Because the "bust" will be over. And who will be here to pick up the pieces of their lives? The residents who steadfastly stood by local merchants during the lean times and they were rewarded with a deaf ear and careless attitude. The power plant that did not bring prosperity, promised jobs and increased taxes to the area? No, they sold a dream that in reality was a nightmare.

People elected to government, whether it be local, state or federal, need to possess vision! Vision for the future, long term answers and protect the most vulnerable among us. That is the pledge they take and the legacy they leave. If the local officials would have done their own research and interviewed citizens who actually live in a power plant town, they may have at least gotten a contract with more money and perks for the town. I am aware of similar contracts which heavily invest in the town, to the tune of millions of dollars! I don't know if they would have "sold out" to the investors and county government agencies so easily. Maybe if they would have listened to the opposition, better deals could have been reached, benefiting many more families and many more lives! But when the mind is closed and ideas are not permitted by those less popular, dialog stops and ignorance sets in. I will always research and dive into facts before forming an opinion. My mother said my first word was "why". If that's the case, I guess I have lived my destiny. It certainly hasn't been easy when you are assaulted daily. You are even threatened and made to look evil in the eyes of many but I can live with that. What I could never live with is that I caused someone harm.

The power plant in Jessup, Pennsylvania is three miles away from communities and yet the citizens are still affected by the bright lights and noise. Personal air filters in their homes become dark with particles and there are several power plant events that should have been investigated by DEP and were not. The power plant must be more honest and deliberate when selling their product. They should not participate in propaganda, false hope and empty promises.

Human beings are designed to understand truth and weigh options but not if the "facts" are hand fed to them or sound too good, they should know it probably is not the truth. We also know when a deal is being sold for the benefit of a few "investors". Everybody jumps on the bandwagon to make a fast buck, live for the present but that is not what is expected from our politicians. We pray that they consider all options and weigh the facts. That they look at the long term and not just the immediate future. Possession of such vision and insight is rare and the people with the gift, often are looked upon with wonder. It is also difficult to be a free thinker and not follow the crowd. No one likes to be ostracized or lonely but blessed are those who bring forth truth. At the time of this writing, another power plant is being considered in another county in Pennsylvania, six times the size of the plant in Renovo. The Pennsylvania government brings power plants to its state and exploits its resources for jobs and money. Much of the energy made in these plants is sold to New York state, where they proudly proclaim that their state is "promoting the green deal" and not contributing to climate change. Wow! Maybe they should just say we don't care about our neighbors to the south as long as we can propagate ideas of grandeur, in the minds of our constituents!

The Green Deal always reverts back to greenbacks and greed. We have not devised a safe way to dispose of windmills without burying them in the soil. We are always reliant on Mother Earth to clean up after us. We annihilate tropical rain forests and expose the barren wastelands, without regard to the humans and animals who need the forest to survive. We detonate and devise new ways to peel into our earth and exploit its minerals and resources until nothing is left to mine or harvest. We did learn some agricultural techniques and lessons from the dust bowl days but we fail to keep up with new technologies and proper disposal methods. Recycling is in its infancy and because we have not yet made it "profitable" we suffer from our ignorance of manufacturing too much waste. It shouldn't be that hard to find profitability in processing waste but it sure doesn't seem to be a priority. In a global economy, with a constant search for new markets, shouldn't a priority be given to how we are going to process the abundance of its packaging? What will happen in fifty years when the power plant closes? We continue to kick the perpetual can down the street and offer no answers. Sadly, after more than a hundred years, we still cannot reconcile our need for things, against our need to protect ourselves or our planet. In the last fifty years, we took giant steps upon the moon and yet baby steps protecting planet earth. As usual, we bankrupt future generations with the problems and debt we create today. Long after we are gone from this world, what will our legacy become? One of wealth over health? One of indifference over compassion? Or will we be grateful that we had full bellies and big bank accounts, with our friends and neighbors as collateral?

The actions of one brave woman, to retain a copy of the DEP report, when explicitly told to destroy it, will always be remembered as a hero. She was an average citizen, wife and mother, who had an extraordinarily difficult life. Most people, when they befall tragedy at a young age, such as sexual assault and molestation, have deep seeded emotions, unwilling to heal. This was before the help of doctors who specialize in healing the mind and offering support. This was before drug therapy and the myriad of pharmaceuticals available today. In her youth, her emotional state was not considered valuable and the 'ole boys club' philosophy was alive and well. You see, boys will be boys and if a young woman was violated, it must have been her fault! Such archaic thinking was despicable and sad but that's truly how it was back then. Even today there is a negative connotation when it comes to discussing mental health. We widely accept addiction as a disease but if you mention mental wellness, you are somehow ostracized and made to feel demonized or shameful.

When she gave birth to children who were off the spectrum, she had no resources or support system. She and her children made their way carefully through the negative stares and dismissive smirks and plodded forward. Their step through each day must have been difficult and comber-some but they prevailed. She didn't easily trust people, which is not hard to figure out why. She was basically alone in the world, raising a family, in spite of the challenges surrounding her.

When she was asked to destroy the DEP report, she in good conscience, could not go through with it. The report identified the mismanagement of the soil and watershed, with dangerous levels of e-coli and fecal matter, along with chemical combinations that were toxic. This contamination occurred by improper sewerage elimination procedures, dating back many years. But she couldn't help but wonder if the contamination had contributed to the birth defects of her children. Or if it was just a cruel trick of nature. Whatever the cause, she was unapologetically committed to keep the report alive and not destroy its message. She cared about her neighbors and community at large and was determined to see that the information in the report would find purpose. Not to save her or her family but to serve others.

There was a neighbor, who had befriended the woman's children and had daily interaction with them. She was generous and kind and the children became friends with her. Although their mother stifled her personal enthusiasm for their growing friendship, she knew that it was a blessing. Her children were thriving and happy with their new companion.But she would remain emotionally distant because that was her comfort zone. Her past had broken her belief in friendships and trust but her children did not have to carry that burden, she carried it alone.

Then one day, there was an enormous, torrential rain that descended upon the mountain area. It swelled the earth beyond its ability to hold any more volume! The poisonous ground swell, unable to hold back its flood waters, cascaded down the mountain into the valley below. In the valley, the waters rose and an unholy alliance was formed. Homes in the valley were flooded, not just with raging new streams but colliding with the water from the mountains above. The flooding seeped then raged into homes and filled them with a mixture of acid mine drainage, e-coli, fecal matter and various chemical compounds.

Homes were contaminated and suffered varying levels of structural disturbance. The waters receded but not all damage disappeared. In fact some of the worse toll on personal health would be forthcoming. As the sun evaporates the moisture and it is wicked away, the sun also dries out the soil and does its best to heal the planet, but the planet cannot heal itself completely, nor can it protect its inhabitants from harm.

Cancer is a pervasive and ravaging illness and doctors use many pervasive and ravaging treatments to cure it in the human body. It is a subtle disease, striking people without warning and offering life changing alterations to a victim's journey in life. Many positive strides have been made in medicine and life expectancy is far better today than at any time in our existence. But it is an intrusive monster that rears its ugly head and strikes out at will. No one is immune from its wrath and many lose their life due to its fury. And so it was that the kind and caring friend of the children would be its next target! Because the high levels of contamination that soaked her home in the valley, had also breached her human defenses. Cancer is the most vicious and invasive mutation to inhabit the human body on a cellular level. In order to eradicate the disease, medicines must kill off good cells as well as the bad. They are developing targeted therapies which do not destroy as much healthy tissue and pinpoint the accuracy of the drug to the disease. The hope is one day cancer can be cured! But for now,we rely on it going into remission and hope it doesn't return.

Our fragile existence is a reminder that we are not invincible. We all may fall victim, at any time to circumstance, our environment, our decisions or destiny. We strive to be a good neighbor, good steward of our gifts and be a great friend. Our relationships are difficult and complex but also rewarding and enlightening. We share this planet with one another and should all be moving in the same direction in concern to pollution and caring for the environment. We lean on the promises of our government to keep us safe, only to find that their services are sold to the highest bidder. Large corporations give lip service to conservation and ecological ideals but in reality talk out both sides of their mouths.

We each have an obligation to leave this planet in better shape than it was in when we inherited it. The lost DEP report would be lost forever if it stayed in the hands of the owner. Time, illness and old age were creeping into her bones and her life was coming to an eventual end. It was time for her to see that her children were well cared for and she would remain in nursing care for the duration of her days. Therefore, the time was now to hand over this report to someone she could trust. But since trust had always been an issue with her, this would not be easy. Who could she pass the torch to that would ensure it would be read and acted upon? She knew it was a powerful tool in getting her community cleaned up and restored. However, there were many forces who wanted to keep the report secret and never see the light of day. It was seen to them, not as a message of environmental responsibility but rather, a roadblock on their way to bring development to this area. I do not know why they opposed a clean up of the area, except that they could not gain control of the project. If a clean up were to take place, then a delay in their plans was inevitable. Their plans were to obtain land and build 4x4 trails to attract tourism dollars. This is a perfectly sound idea, except they were determined to locate trails where they intended, not necessarily where they were wanted.

Capitalism is not always patient or discreet and the desire to build this robust trail throughout Pennsylvania and connecting to New York would be expensive.

The very existence of this report was a time-bomb. Who do you hand a time-bomb off to? Someone who cares about health over wealth and a clean environment over profits. Someone who had displayed their kindness and compassion to her children. Someone who could take a hold of the baton and finish the race. And so she did, hand off the report and by doing so, inadvertently put the recipient's life in danger.

Profits can stand in the way of one's compassion for their fellow man. We are told we cannot serve two gods and that is very applicable in this case. The same individuals who told the report holders to destroy their copies, were some of the same individuals investing in creating the 4x4 trails. In fact, they became well placed individuals within their community and at the county level. They served on several committees and became a network, using the power of politics and cash as their weapons of choice. Always selling the benefit of their plans without allowing for discussion or any dissent. They carefully selected their army of compliant and obedient servants and even allowed them to invest in their vision. But at no time did absolute control ever leave the hands of a few! Power and intimidation became law and anyone who possessed a different point of view or had a competing thought was immediately marked as an enemy. Because of their emboldened status within the community, they seemed untouchable. But no one is above or beyond the grasp of law-abiding citizens who feel a moral obligation to serve their community. These individuals are powerful in their own right and when they bring honest and forthright concerns to bear and also have the law on their side, they can be invincible!

The 4x4 trails innovative thinkers and the investors of a defunct, bankrupt business, were destined to meet and collaborate! And this happened when a power plant, to be built in the center of Renovo upon the land owned by investors, came together! This marriage was not made in heaven. You had the expertise of manipulators able to entice and seduce willing investors. Since the DEP report had disappeared, years before, they discussed how they would manipulate the DEP's attention away from another toxic waste site, sell the land and reap the financial rewards. The land the investors owned was the old railroad property and it had been the site of several businesses after the railroad closed. With state and local investment dollars, businesses sprouted up and after they made their profits and would be obligated to start repaying tax dollars, they closed! Renovo had been the ongoing victim to these get rich quick schemes but the victims were the employees, left to be unemployed time and time again. No one seems to consider the fate of these people and the tremendous highs and lows they may have lived. After a while, the roller coaster of emotions is too hard to ride and they may turn to soothing their pain. Not all choices they make are healthy ones but when your life has been in free fall, any mind numbing methods are welcomed.

The division of the haves and have nots has been created. The perpetual unemployed could not afford the ten thousand dollar minimum investment in the investors club. Membership was closed to the disenfranchised and derelict. Only successful men and women could be members of this club and the prestige and satisfaction they felt was addicting!

The 4x4 trails innovators now had an alliance with the investors and by merging these two powerful groups, nothing could get in their way! But many of the forty-nine investors did not recognize that their vision was hijacked. All they were interested in was trying to recoup some of their initial investment. Most investors do not get a second chance and with the prospect of the power plant coming to town, and infusion of cash, jobs and tax dollars, they felt like they had just hit the trifecta at a horse race!

If you are an astute investor, you do your research on your investment. In the case of these investors, they would have made out better by backing a filly. The figurehead of these negotiations with the power plant was a failed businessman and an assortment of politicians. In the world of successful businesses, true negotiations are done by competent and knowledgeable individuals. Ones who have researched for themselves the scope of the project, the true benefit to the community and the willingness to address concerns. However, this was not the case because the innovators had acted in secrecy all these years, moving piece by piece on a chessboard of their own creation. They were not willing to share facts with the investors and only spoon fed them tidbits of information, as necessary to appease their appetite. For the most part, the investors were satisfied and as the years of negotiations with the power plant went virtually undetected by many in Renovo. It was exhilarating to be a part of a secret plan, where you were going to get a second chance at getting back some of your investment dollars! So what if a power plant was dropped into the middle of town. Only a handful of investors actually lived in Renovo, so they were not bothered by the fact that many of their friends and neighbors were going to be living with a power plant, within feet of their home! All the real decisions of the power plant were done at the county level because Renovo chose not to have their own planning commission. There were no votes taken in reference to the power plant by the voters or even the Renovo Borough Council.

All decisions were taken out of their hands and directly into the hands of others. Renovo was taken over and all decision power taken from them and the residents. It was a silent takeover and left them in defeat but they never really noticed. It was slick and perfectly orchestrated until the woman with the "missing DEP report" and a writer met. Cancer survivor, veteran, mental health/community worker, foster parent, all these attributes wrapped up into one compassionate person. And she was in possession of the missing DEP report! That made her fear for her life, at times, especially when she was aware of just how corrupt and the innovators were, especially when it came to buying up desired properties. Properties that would connect the 4x4 trails and bring sustained profitability to a select few. She read the report and was horrified by its contents, could this all really be true? So she spent the next several years corresponding, investigating, researching, taking water and soil samples for testing and yes, it was all true! DEP and DCNR officials being misdirected, corruption of the law and indignity to fellow citizens. Years of notes, documents, correspondence and uncovering the truth about the soil contamination of the past and never cleaned up.

The story of two brave women who for entirely different reasons but both motivated by conviction, would someday have their story told. It is also the story of an eclectic bunch of people who questioned the wisdom of placing a power plant in the center of a town. But what about Renovo? Will the power plant be built on the toxic waste site? Did the coming together of citizens from a small town in Jessup, sharing their power plant journey with three from Renovo, give them enough information to make a difference?

**To Be Continued…**

Maureen is a former, business woman, concerned citizen, wife, mother, sister, aunt and best friend. She loves painting, gardening, photography, attending meetings with the Chapman Wordweavers Society, mentoring and volunteering her time assisting abused children.